The Power of Purpose

Written by: Pixie Lee

Published by Bizzy Bossy Mommy

Marietta, GA

Cover design by Milos Jevremovic

Copyright 2018 by Pixie Lee

First printing December 2017

All rights reserved. No part of this book may be reproduced in any form or by any means without permission in writing from the author.

ISBN: 978-1983408205

Printed USA

Table of Contents

Introduction: ……………………………………….page 11

Chapter 1: What Is Purpose?…………………………... page 15

Chapter 2: The Road Traveled……………………….page 23

Chapter 3: Lightbulb Moment…………..…………….page 36

Chapter 4: What Now? ……………………………..page 50

Chapter 5: Setbacks……………………...…….……page 63

Chapter 6: I'm Still Searching, It's Ok To Say No………page 71

Chapter 7: What Have We Learned?…………………….page 83

Foreword

The aim of The Power of Purpose is to motivate the reader to do so much more than meander through life wondering "Why am I here? What should I be doing? What is God's plan and purpose for my life?"

I pray that God will use The Power of Purpose to allow every person who reads it to set and achieve meaningful goals so that each person will know what he or she is not here only to be another number in the population. May God use this work to aid and assist you with the finding his purpose for your life so that you will know with crystal clear clarity exactly why you are here. Be blessed by the new territory of purpose.

Rev. R. L. Glover

Dedication

This book is dedicated to the memory of my grandparents: Estella and Ernest Glover, Sr., Walter Cottonham, Grace Johnson, and to my niece, Grace McKenzie (Midget). There isn't a day that goes by that I don't think of you and miss you. I carry each of you with me daily. It is my hope that you are proud of the things I've done and accomplished.

I love you.

Acknowledgements

There are so many people I need to thank. First and foremost, I want to the God for the vision he entrusted in me. I always knew I wanted to write a book, and I'm glad this was the vision and plan that God had for me. Completing this book was not only life changing, it was eye opening.

I want to thank my parents. We always wait until we are standing over a person's casket to express how much a person means, I want my parents to know while they can hear me. I want them to know how much I love them and appreciate them. No matter what business venture or new excursion, I have embarked on, they have always been there to support me. They never discourage me from trying new things and stepping out on faith. They have always had my back and have always shown up for me, and I will always show up and have theirs. There isn't anything in this world that I wouldn't do for them. There is no amount of money that will ever be sufficient to repay the unwavering support and love I have received from them. They have given me the strong spiritual foundation and been as close to the model parent as they could. They have shown me what hard work will do and how to be a great parent to my own children. I hope to continue to make them proud in everything that I do.

To my wonderful business bestie, Coach Aj: I will never forget the day I walked in for training and upon hearing you speak; I knew I was in the right place and on the right path. I thank you for your knowledge and wisdom on this journey to not only completing this book but helping me in this Life Coaching business. You are truly a God sent angel and I am eternally grateful.

I have to thank my friends. I have had so many talks with all of them on different topics; they were my guinea pigs. We have cried and yelled, and they have let me bounce ideas off of them. I practiced on them until I got it right. It means a lot to be able to have people in your corner that trusts you with their lives and their deepest darkest secrets and fears. And for them to trust you enough to seek your help and take your advice, it is priceless.

To my best friend, Lucy (Treecie): We have seen each other through some good times, bad times, difficult times and all the ones in the middle. Life has thrown us some curve balls we never saw coming. But we've gotten through them together. All we need is a friends marathon and by the end, we have it all figured out. I love you!

And Crash: You have listened to ideas, and given advice, let me panic and scream when it wasn't even necessary. I appreciate you and our friendship more than you will ever know.

To the horseman: Randi, Jared, Brandon and Drea! My siblings rock! We have the best conversations when we all get together. Not even geography can change our relationship. I truly appreciate you guys pushing me and loving me and believing in me. I wouldn't trade any of you for the world.

To my Uncle Clark: You keep me laughing. I truly enjoyed the conversations we had in the living room.

To Felix: Although there is an age gap between us, I feel like we grew up together. We have learned a lot about life and each other over the years. We have our ups and downs along with our disagreements, but I thank you for showing up for our children and for supporting them in their school activities, after school activities and their dreams. I appreciate you putting their needs, wants, desires and happiness above anything else that may come. I am truly grateful to be able to co parent our children together. I thank you for supporting me and being my friend.

Being at one place for 30 plus years, you have some friends who become family. To all my young adults: You have grown into amazing people. You have shared some of the most personal and private moments of your lives with me. We have laughed, cried, fussed and everything in the middle. I watch you now and I am so happy how things are turning out. I know there are a lot of good things to come; I thank you for allowing me to be a part of that.

Then there are the little people in my life: My niece, Jellybean (Aniyah), my nephew, Snoopy (Grayson), my god-daughter, Moonpie (Gabrielle), and my god-son, Tookieman (Kaiden). It is my esteem pleasure to be on this journey of life with you. I love all you with all my heart. I am always here no matter when times are good or bad, I will always be in your corner and I will always have your back.

And last but not least, my 3 heart beats: Briah, Maya and Cameron: my crew. You are my greatest achievement. I can't begin to imagine what my life would be like without the 3 of you. You are my reason for everything that I do. I want to leave a legacy that will bless you, your children, and your future. I want you to know the importance of a spiritual relationship and a strong family foundation. Life can be ugly, but I want you to always remember that no matter what mommy is here. I will be here to share in your accomplishments, wipe tears from your eyes, give advice when needed, both solicited and unsolicited. There will never be a day that you will ever have to wonder because mommy is always here. From the first time I looked in all of your eyes and held you in my arms, it created a bond that can never be broken. I am so thankful for the loving and fun relationships that I have with each of you. You make me proud to call you my children and I am honored daily as we navigate through this game called life.

Introduction

This book has been in the making for the last couple of years. I knew several years ago, I wanted to write a book, and God confirmed that for me. I never knew what that book was going to be about, but then I received my answer after the last two years of my life. They haven't been easy, but I knew my story was one that I wanted to share. I knew it was one that would help someone else. I've always been the person who people come to for advice and to bounce ideas off of when making decisions or a big change, but it took me a minute to figure out that was my calling and what I was supposed to be doing. So now that I've found it, let's get started.

Have you ever found yourself wondering what am I doing here? Have you prayed and asked God for something and he granted your request in order to prove to you what he already knew? This isn't what you need my child. Are you wondering what you need to do in order to find complete satisfaction? Do you keep going to school to get new degrees and certificates only to find no satisfaction in that area either? If you answered yes to any of these questions, then you are in the right book, and you're in for a treat. This book is to help those who feel like they are walking in the dark. Whether it's the corporate working person who hates their job and gets no satisfaction from being there or the person that knows there is something bigger and better that they are supposed to be doing but don't know what it is. In this book, we are going to dig deep inside of ourselves and take the mask off and go down to the bare bones of life. We'll remove the layers that have been weighing you down, allowing for healing and accomplishment while taking what you look at as tragedy and turn it into triumph.

This book is a step-by-step process to walk you through the process to find what your purpose is. Unearthing the reason for your being, while finding the answers to your missing questions, and getting on the path you were meant to walk. Before you read the next page, stop, breathe and repeat this prayer.

Lord, I thank you for your many blessings. I thank you for being who you are and who you are in my life. God, I ask that you open my mind, my heart and my eyes. I am looking to find the reason you created me. I am looking for my purpose in life. I ask that you be with me in this process. Show me what I need to see, lead, guide and direct my path. I thank you for clarity, direction, and understanding. In Jesus name, I pray, Amen.

Now, let's take this walk, shall we? You will need paper, pen, and a highlighter. We want to dig into ourselves and get some answers. I pray that God speaks to you in a way that you have never heard his voice before. I hope that by the end of this book, you not only have your purpose, but a renewed energy, fire, and desire inside to unleash on the world.

SOMETHING GREAT IN YOUR FUTURE.
ISAIAH 43:19

"My mama sent me an email this morning to remind me we have to stand on God's promises. There is not a time that we face difficulty and God doesn't see our struggle, our pain, or our tears. We have to go through the difficulty to go to the other side of it. We will appreciate what God has in store for us because of what we endured to get it. Psalms 121 says I will lift up mine eyes unto the hills from whence cometh my help. My help cometh from the Lord. Don't always expect the help to be financial. That help could be strength, peace, comfort, love or someone to remind you of the goodness of Jesus. He is a great God; even when all hell is breaking loose around us. He still deserves our praise, even when we think there is nothing to praise him for. We owe him a praise just for who he is! Praise your way through! See your answer. See your victory! Your time is coming!"

Chapter 1: What Is Purpose?

If you haven't gotten your paper by now, this would be a good time. We are going to make some notes as we take this journey together. So, the first things first, I want you to write three things that you are good at. This could be cooking, singing, writing, or anything that you are good at. Now, let's write down what is your favorite thing to do? Between your favorite thing to do and these three things that you are good at, is this something you do daily? Would you prefer to do this than what you are paid to do on a daily basis? Can you see yourself turning one of these things into a business? While we let that marinate, let's keep this train moving.

The first place to start would be for us to actually define purpose. What does it mean? What is purpose? Dictionary.com defines purpose in two ways. One way is as a noun with the meaning the reason for which someone exists or is done, made, used, etc. It also defines it as a verb with the meaning to intend or design. Now while that may not strike you, let me give you my definition.

My definition of purpose is the reason God created me and the special gift he gave me. When God created us, he had a specific thing in mind. He knew what our lives would be like. He arranged things the exact way he needed to in order to get the desired results. Now while that sounds like really great, there is a problem. The problem is some of us have made some decisions, which has caused God to allow certain things to happen to us in order to get us back on track. Is it a bad thing? This all depends on your perspective. I'm sure at some point we would all say yes these things that have happened to us are bad things. However, think about it from the other side. If this particular bad thing had not happened, what about your life would be different? Would you think the same way that you do now? Would you look at life the same way that you do? Probably not. We must take the lesson and use it as a building block to go higher.

We aren't meant to stay in one place. Think of life as a board game, not necessarily the game of Life, just your own board game if you will. If you're traveling down Opportunity Boulevard and instead of crossing over the bridge of hardships, you take a left down

Wallow Lane, would you get the same outcome? Maybe eventually but maybe not. If you're playing a board game, the end result is to win the game. However, depending on the path that is taken, that will determine if you win, or if you make it to the end at all.

"If you can't figure out your purpose, figure out what your passion. For your passion will lead you right into your purpose" - **Bishop T.D. Jakes**

Your thoughts have become audible. I can hear you saying, "Do you have a purpose?" And the answer is yes. You may not know what your purpose is, but there is something there that you have been called to do. You are special in your own way. You have something within in you that only you can do the way you do it. It is what you have been born to do. For example, I've been in several multi-level marketing companies. From juice to water to weight loss, and on and on and so forth and so forth. What I noticed in every meeting that I attended is there was always someone who was the featured guest. I'm sure you've been to a meeting as well. So you know what I'm talking about. This special guest is the "top earner" in the company. They have broken records and just amazed the owners. They were supposed to the expert on either multi-level marketing or this particular product. Now when they take the stage, they have a message. They have something that they want to get over to me. I sat there anxiously waiting to hear what the big secret was. As I sat there, I would think to myself and laugh because I know me. *I can do that. I can do what they are doing, and I could probably do it better.* I know there is a way I could command a room, there was a way that I spoke, that would engage people. I could get them to believe in a product just like I did. It was at that time that I realized there is only one me!

You may be able to do what I do, but you can't do it like I do it. It's not being boisterous; it's being honest. It's being confident. It's tapping into who you are and recognizing the gift that is within you. <u>Nobody can be a better you.</u> When you're trying to be something or someone that you aren't, you lose the essence of you—the core and that special light that makes you special.

So I ask you now, what makes you special? Make a list of the things that you bring to the table. And these things make up the best, honest, and confident YOU!!! The best YOU!! The you that everyone envies. The you that everyone wants to be. The YOU that knows what they want and is making the plan of action to go get it and get it DONE!

Finding and working in your purpose gives your life a new meaning. A light shines around you, and when you begin to speak, people can tell that this is what you're supposed to be doing. Some people may already know what your purpose is, but you might not be receptive or ready for it. There are also those of us who didn't want to hear it because it's not what we wanted to do. Well, let me tell you now. It's not about what you want to do; it's what you were CALLED to do. It's no different from a person running from their calling to be a minister. For most people, it's not easy. People run and avoid it, and God literally has to knock them down before they give up and say "Ok God, I get it and I'll go." Even though your calling may not be in ministry, it's no difference when you're looking for your purpose. We get a glimpse, but because it's not what we want it to be or what we want to do, we keep going. And God is so funny, that he will let us keep running in circles until he probably entertains himself. Knowing in the end, we will be back to this starting point, we walk aimlessly through life with what seems like a million questions and no answers. We create some tough roads that we didn't have to walk, but they all have one path and lead back to one point. Your purpose.

I've always said I know God has a sense of humor because he made me. I'm funny, and a lot of fun to be around. I love to laugh and tell jokes. Nevertheless, I know being a comedian isn't what I am supposed to be doing. You're simply laughing at my point of view of life with this extra sauciness of wicked entertainment. See how I just described why I like having fun? And no one will ever describe it like that again. So you see we all have something about us that stand out makes people want to be around us. I want you to think about what that is. And while you're thinking, we'll take a look back at the last two years of my life that brought us to the point of writing this book to help you find what you're looking for.

Three Things You Are Good At Helping others strive towards their potential
Encouraging others
1. Making others feel good about themselves
2. Working w/ others as a team
3. Problem-solving, making plans and trying to follow them step by step

Your Favorite Thing to Do

1. Be in nature

Notes

Chapter 2: The Road Traveled

So I know at this point you're wondering what my purpose is, and how did I get there? Well let me tell you, it has not been an easy road to travel. Life has taught me some hard lessons and some of which I probably could have avoided. I was about as hardheaded as they come. When I graduated high school, I knew going to college was the next logical step. However, I can't say that I was excited about it. It was almost as if I was forced even though I wasn't. All my parents said was go and I did. I applied at Chattahoochee Tech after Kennesaw State denied my application. I was so heartbroken. I had a feeling of not being good enough, and I said I was going to work and reapply, and the next time I was getting in. In the meantime, I had to go to plan B, which at the time didn't exist. Someone told me to apply to Chattahoochee Tech, so I did. I finished all my paperwork, walked into financial aid, and was told I couldn't get any grants for college without a program of study. Let me take you into this train of thought that left that station. See, I figured if I did general studies and passed all my classes then when I reapplied at Kennesaw State, they would take me, and then I would figure out what I wanted to do with my life. HA! That was not how that was going down that day. I asked the lady behind the counter for help, and she was real nice when she told me this was my decision. I thought, *Oh Lord, what am I going to do?* I couldn't call and ask mama and daddy because they would tell me I would have to decide what I wanted to do. Therefore, I did the next best thing. I asked for a catalog.

Now while I'm standing here trying to figure out my life in 30 seconds or less, with a line full of people behind me, I opened the book, and the first program on there was Accounting. I replied, "Put me in that." She said very well, updated my file, and I was off to the races. My checklist was shaping up real nice. I had applied to school, gotten accepted, selected a program of study, and I had financial aid for school because, at this point, that was my goal for the day. I did have a job, and for an 18-year old that lived at home, with minimal bills it paid very well, just not well enough to pay for school. So my goal for the day had been accomplished, and it was on to the next step. I went on to get my schedule and books, and now it was just time for the first day of school. What was funny to me was when people asked me what I was going to school for and I said accounting, some weren't surprised, and yet I couldn't even tell you what I was getting ready to embark on. I didn't know any accountants. I never said I want to be a CPA when I grow up. Heck by this time, I had only filed a tax return once and didn't know that fell under accounting. Nevertheless, the reason no one was surprised is, while sitting at my desk and working, I would balance my checkbook over three times a day and redo my budget to pay bills at least twice. What no one realized was my ultimate goal was to make sure all the bills were paid, and I had some extra money left over. That was also one reason my budget and checkbook was in pencil, lol. So being in accounting and working with numbers wasn't too farfetched. It was just never my dream job.

  I completed the first quarter of school before I decided it was time for a break. You remember the bridges and left turns I talked about earlier? Well, here was my first of many left turns. I left school, took a break, and began to live a life. It wasn't necessarily the one I was supposed to live, but it was chop full of lessons that would serve me greatly in the years to come.

As I'm living life, I began to make some bad decisions—some that would have a negative impact on me. I ended up losing my first apartment and moving back home, but I was dating my high school sweetheart again. Life was pretty ok at this point. As you can see, it didn't take long for me to start taking the long way around. I wouldn't listen, and I figured I had it all under control. I the 18-year-old, with a full-time job who only completed one quarter, not even a semester, had life figured out and could do it without guidance and assistance. Well, again, I'm living life, and my oldest daughter was born soon after I moved back home my sweetheart, and I broke up, and I was making more life-changing decisions. Only this time, I was responsible for someone else's life. The day I told my dad I was pregnant, I was on the verge of quitting my job. Needless to say, the first thing he said after I already knew that was, keep your butt on that job. It was not what I wanted to hear, but I did. And after I got the bills for the doctor, hospital, and birth, I was glad I did. Sheesh. Now the decisions I made had a greater impact than just me and my life, and as life began to happen, I met my husband. He wasn't my favorite person upon us meeting, but I wasn't his either. There were not rockets going off, and it wasn't love at first sight.

Nevertheless, we began dating, got engaged, and had a daughter and a couple of years later a son. So now I'm married, with three kids, working and I decided well, it's time to finish this degree. It didn't dawn on me at the time that this was not going to be an easy accomplishment. It didn't dawn on me that family life and work life would take priority, and there would be sometimes that I would be up while everyone was sleeping because I made the decision to leave after the first quarter. Hmmm, I should have thought that through, but I didn't.

I talked to my husband, and he said, "Ok cool. I got you." Now this time around, I was considering changing my major. Here goes another one of those twists and turns in the board game of my life. I was working in a group home for boys ages 15-21 and I thought that's what I wanted to do with my life. I thought helping these young men become productive people in society was my calling, and I was pretty good at it. I was a mama 24/7, not only at home but at work too. I went to schools, jobs, shopping, had life skills training with these guys, graduations, doctor appointments, and everything else they needed me to do. I was the mama of the house, and it seemed like a good fit until it wasn't. I knew when it was time for me to leave, but me being the hardheaded dummy I was, I stayed.

So when God was tired of me not doing what he said, he made me leave. When I left that job, I went back to school and finished my degree in Accounting. Yeah, Accounting; I guess you can see by now, I just didn't have this thought process together.

While working in the group home, I made a connection with the bookkeeper at the time. She and I became friends, and she introduced me to her uncle and her aunt, and my life in accounting began. Who knew my degree would come in handy so quickly? I certainly didn't. I began doing taxes and learning more on the job than I did in any classroom. I managed to hook up with a CPA that was not afraid to teach me anything. He shared his knowledge daily. After working with him in his company and moving around to different offices, I decided I would open my own office. I would talk to my parents all the time about having my own. They told me long before I actually did it, that I could do it. They had more confidence in me than I had in myself.

Working under the CPA and his brand was safe. I could call at any time I needed help, and he was always there. He impressed upon me to continuously read and be trained. But, he was teaching the class so again it was safe. It wasn't that I didn't believe my parents; I was just scared to walk out there and do it. Cutting the safety net can be a scary thing. But you have to get in the deep end to see if you're going to sink or swim. I'm proud to say I was able to swim.

For the first time, I was doing something that I loved and as the song says, "I did it my way" LOL! Life was good for a while. I was able to accomplish a lot of things, and I absolutely enjoyed the freedom of making my own hours. Then life happened again, and I had to make some big girl decisions. These decisions were even harder this time around for many different reasons. For one, I was now responsible for four lives— mine and my three children. I had to decide what would be the best road to take. Do I stay at my own company that is having some financial issue or do I do it on a part-time basis and go get a full-time job? Can I weather the storm and get back to an even ground? How long is this going to last? Where will I end up if I don't cut my losses now? My children need a roof over their heads, clothes on their back, and food in their stomach. I guess you're looking at this wondering why I only counted four lives, right. Well, one of the roads I had to travel was divorce. My husband and I were no longer together, and there was no one to go home and talk to but God. I talked with my parents, and they gave the best advice they could, but never once did they make the decision for me. It wasn't what they wanted me to do; it was what I needed to do for me and my family. And that's exactly what I did. I was a mom first, and I did the only logical thing I could do. I went and got a job and decided to work my business on a part-time basis. It took a little longer than anticipated, but I did it. I had a horrible job that made you question why that company was even opened. But it was a stepping-stone to where I wanted to be anyway. I was hired at The Home Depot.

This job was life-changing for so many reasons. I met some very awesome people who are dear to me. I was able to do what I needed to do, and that was providing for my family. And it was also at this job that I had my lightbulb moment. Now it wasn't something that I embraced upon hearing it. I heard it and was like umm nah, that's not me. I had a friend who called me one day on the way to work. I had a friend riding with me, and while I was on the phone, her wheels were turning.

When I got off the phone, she said, "You should be a life coach. They make really good money."

"Life coach? What is that? What do they do?" I said.

Our conversation continued, and I must admit I was intrigued. I started doing my research online and who knew you could get paid helping people and you weren't a doctor. I thought about it for about seven days and said nope. I'm good. Let's pause for a second, so here I am taking yet another detour. Why, why, and more why? Why must things be so hard? I'm sure God was like this nut right here. I dropped it right in her lap, but because the earth didn't move and windows didn't shake, she misses what I have for her.

That was my million-dollar mistake! There it was right before my eyes, and I walked away from it. I didn't give it much thought; I just said no. I looked at stuff online for about an hour a day in this week, and I called that doing "research". What in world could I have really found inside that hour? Ugh, can we say nothing! I told my mom what was said to me, and she said "huh". Not that she didn't hear me but kinda more so like hmm really? To this day I don't know if she was saying yes do it, or if she was as confused as I was.

We look for confirmation from familiar sources that we trust, and when we don't get the answer we are seeking, then we decide that must mean they didn't agree. She never disagreed; she just didn't give me the green light. At 36 years old, I was still looking for confirmation that I was on the right track. I'm sure I'm not the only one who still talks to their parents or that person you trust to get the seal of approval. It was ok. It was easier to go back to work the next day and just leave that right there. The seed had been planted, but that was all. It stayed in the back of my head, and I didn't act on it—at least not just yet.

Love the life you live, live the life you love

"We have to be thankful for the things we have! Your life is your life! What is it about your life you want to change? What is missing? Don't look at the material things! Those can change at the drop of a hat! You hate your job? Let's find another one! You want to be self-employed? Take a class and see what you need to do to be the best at it?? New car? Go test drive and make a plan! But most of all do you have a meaningful relationship with God?? He's the answer to everything. Material things will come and go, but his love, peace, presence, and comfort is everlasting! Let go of what you think is the problem! Let go of the people that cause that pain! Your happy place is with the Lord! And it doesn't have to be dead to enjoy it! Live on purpose! Live the life he has for you and love the life you have! It's not all sunshine, but it is all happiness and joy!"

Notes

Chapter 3: The Lightbulb Moment

Months went by after I had this conversation and things began to happen. Here comes another left turn. This one was way more serious than the others I had taken. This one involved my health. On June 28, 2016, I got the worse migraine of my life. It was so bad that I couldn't function. I couldn't get it to go away for anything. All the things that I would normally do weren't working. I drank the Pepsi with something sweet and laid down. Nothing. I took meds after meds and laid down. Still nothing. I even went to the emergency room, and that's something I don't do. I've suffered from migraines since I was 16 years old, so I knew what worked and what to do. So, for me to go the emergency room, it was bad. They gave me the migraine cocktail, and I slept the next 24 hours right on away. When I woke up, I still had this migraine. Only this time it was back with a vengeance. By now, we are going into week three of this migraine. I had cried, and cried, and cried. And three weeks later, I'm still in pain.

My sister came over to my apartment with all these remedies for self-healing and pain relief the natural way, and although the cider was great and the aromatherapy smelled amazing, it didn't work. I'm still hurting. I truly believe now looking back on that migraine that was God trying to get my attention. You remember I had already walked away from what he was trying to tell me. So, at this point, the earth had to move. And I promise you; it was moving. The first day of school has rolled around, and I still have this headache. Needless to say, my entire family is concerned that something bigger is going on, so back to the emergency room I went. I remember lying in the hospital on my second trip crying asking, "Why won't my head stop hurting?" This headache had taken over my life for over a month now.

After speaking with my doctor, it was back to the neurologist I went. I was so frustrated and upset because I had been headache free for two years. And now I'm back to the drawing board. I never thought during that time, that this was God trying to get my attention. I just kept going. I made an appointment with my neurologist, and the fight began. I am screaming for an

MRI, and they were refusing to do one. However, with the symptoms I had, the time frame and I'm sure my attitude, they finally gave in. On November 5, 2016, I had my MRI done. My headache is gone finally, but I was so sick. I could barely walk. I was weak in the knees, sweating profusely and felt nauseated like no other. I went across the street to Walgreens to get something for the nausea. I got something for heartburn too. I was having a horrible time, but I knew I had to get home, and I was not close. I called my mom, talked to her for a minute, and got myself together enough to drive home. I didn't want to scare her since I was on the other side of town. I went straight to my parents' house, fell asleep on the sofa, and that's where I was for the night. The next couple of days were awful. I had no energy. I couldn't eat, couldn't sleep, and guess what was back? Yep, my migraine was back. I worked so hard to get rid of it that I cried that it was back. Again, I'm not looking at this as a sign. I'm still asking why??

I called the doctor back, and the nurse said, "Well, it sounds like you're allergic to the contrast from the MRI."

I immediately got angry. Here I am sick as a dog for days, and this is what the problem was?

The nurse says, "All you need is some milk of magnesia. They should have told you that when you signed in for the MRI."

Now let's look at this logically shall we? If I had been told that I needed to take some milk of magnesia, don't you think I would have bought some when I went in Walgreens? Right!
Out of all the stuff I did purchase and take, that was not one of the items on the list.

I immediately went to CVS, purchased some, and took it. It was the worse tasting stuff on the planet might I add, but I started to feel better. After a second dose, I was almost back to normal. Now while I'm waiting for my results from the MRI, I'm still not looking at this as a sign. I am still not asking God the right questions. I get the results of my MRI, and the left side of my brain is enlarged with fluid. This wasn't the best news to hear and it was very scary. At that moment, all I could think about was my children. Nothing can be wrong with me; I have to be here for them. The doctor was talking, and I missed most of it while I zoned out. She asked if I was ok and tears immediately filled my eyes. So, we went over it again. I called my parents in the parking lot and told them what she said. They were startled and taken aback. I sat in the car and just cried.

It wasn't necessarily the worse news I could have gotten, but it wasn't the best either. Over the next couple of weeks, I scheduled my appointment to have the next procedure done, completed my paperwork for Human Resources and began to deal with this latest health debacle.

I didn't share the news with too many people; I just went on my way. Looking back on this, I could have saved myself a lot of time, pain, and tears had I just asked God, "What are you trying to tell me?" Being the hardheaded pain in the butt that I am, I didn't.

I had the procedure done, and again another left turn. Now I'm having setbacks. The pain was unbearable, and it landed me back in the hospital. This time I had to stay overnight. I talked to my children, reassured them mommy was ok and would be home by the time they got home from school and attempted to sleep. I've never spent the night in the hospital unless I was in the maternity ward, so it was different. It was very uncomfortable. I laid there and stared at the TV, and I was ready to go home as soon as I got the room. I had all this time for God to speak to me, and still, I hadn't said anything to him. I made left turn after left turn, and I haven't asked him one question. I hadn't said one word.

When we get into these sticky situations, a normal person would say, "God, why me? What am I missing?" And I've had those questions and that conversation with God, but for some reason, I never had it this time. I've learned that you don't ask why me, you ask yourself, "Why not me?" You're built for this. You can handle anything that comes your way. You just have to dig down within yourself and use what's inside you. You've been equipped for this all your life. You've got all the tools that you need. No matter if it is sermon notes, conversations, or those good ole fashion talks with an elderly person. You have it, whatever it may be. You've prayed and cried, and here you are at that moment where you can apply those things inside you, and you're not. What are you waiting for?

For me, the writing was on the wall long before this overnight stay, but I hadn't been reading what the wall was saying. I was so blind. Just walking in the dark and moving around without a destination. These endless trips we take in life are so unnecessary sometimes. We pack our bags, begin traveling with no destination in sight, and just walk through life with sunglasses on all the time. We are making all these left turns that aren't really a circle, and we haven't stopped and asked God, "Hey, what am I doing wrong? What should I be doing? Or what do you want me to do?"

We get so tied up in our own thoughts and ideas that we don't realize that everything isn't for us. There is always a reason why things don't work. What you see working for someone else, doesn't necessarily mean it's going to work for you in the same manner. That's one of the things I've always disliked about multi-level marketing. We get caught up in doing it exactly like our leaders because this is what worked for them, and we are upset that it didn't work for us in the same manner.

Did it ever occur to you that they are walking in their purpose? Yeah, there is that pesky word again. This is what they have been called and created to do? This isn't you! You may be able to see yourself on stage, but what are you saying? What are you doing? What direction are you headed in? You may be sitting there in order to get a bigger picture. If it's not your blessing, don't make it your ministry.

I was out of work recovering for the next six to eight weeks. While I was out recovering, I finally got part of the picture. I knew then I had to go back to working for myself. I had to open my business back up on a full-time basis. Over the year that I had been at Home Depot, I had missed a lot of things with my kids, and it was just the worse feeling in the world. My oldest daughter came to me and said I have something coming up at school, but I know you have to work. She wasn't upset, but I was. My heart sank. It was something about not being able to be there and having to request time off that really burned me up on the inside. No one could understand the importance of being there for my kids. No supervisor or manager would understand that I put my kids first no matter what after all they were my kids.

Some people were used to missing things with their kids, but I wasn't. This was one of the biggest adjustments I had to make. I couldn't explain it to myself, so of course; I had problems explaining it to my kids. They were more understanding than I was. But I knew at that moment that I had to show up for them. I had to make the changes needed to be there for them. So while I could only see half the room, I saw enough to know a plan had to be put back in action. As I was getting ready to return to work the following week, I got a phone call that changed the game completely.

My supervisor called me and said, "I have something to tell you. I couldn't let you come back without letting you know what's been going on."

We had a long shocking conversation, but it was the kick in the pants that I needed. The next day I received a call from my general manager. I had never heard him sound like that.

He says to me, "LaQuellis, we have made the decision to close YOW, and you're going to be laid off."

I was really ok with it. I'm probably the only person that was ok with it. I had already gone back to the drawing board when I was sick in December, so I had made the adjustments I needed to make. Still, I looked at several things. I had tried to get on at Home Depot for years to no avail, but I knew a person who referred me. So when I got hired, I was good, and then things started changing. You remember in the beginning I asked you if you have ever asked God for something and he gave it to you because he needed to show you that wasn't for you. Yep, this is my time at Home Depot. Now don't get me wrong, it is a good company to work for, but when you have been called to do something else, and there is a higher calling on your life, mediocracy will never be enough for you. You will always have to excel and go to the next level. I already knew what I was ready to work my plan to get back to my own business opening. I'm sure he thought to himself, she is taking this really well, but I already knew my days were numbered.

Not because of the layoff but because I knew it was time to get back to me. I wasn't going to lose me by making someone else rich. It was time to walk in my passion.

So, I went back to work with 90 days on the calendar until my position was going to be eliminated. I was probably the only one out of all the people in my department that didn't have a complete and total breakdown. There was one young lady that got sick at work and ended up in the hospital, but that wasn't me at all. I knew I had 90 days to get a plan— a workable plan. It was time to put pen to paper and let's rock.

I was talking to another co-worker, and he asked what my plan was? Was I going to apply with the company or what was my next step? I told him I was going to open my company up. It was time to do what I love. He asked what was that. Most people would think at this point, I was going back to accounting, but my answer was different. I said I wanted to help people. He asked how? I said I wasn't sure. I was building a credit business, so I just knew that was my avenue. I told him about the previous conversation I had about being a life coach. He replied that's what you should be doing. I was speechless at that moment because I didn't see it. But I promise you my response THIS time was much different than it was the first time.

So here we are again at this doorstep. Now two different people have said the same thing not knowing what the other one has said. By this time, almost six months had gone by. Let's stop and think about this for a second shall we? How many times have we let things continue only to come back and realize how much time we have wasted? How long you could have or should have been doing something? Have you just gotten so angry with yourself about making a decision that you should have made a long time ago? Yeah, that's where I was, but this time was different. I went back to my mom and started seriously considering it. I started reading and researching for real. This time I wasn't looking for confirmation. I was just letting my mom know I was changing courses. I'm sure she thought to herself, "again". Yes again. The part of my journey that I left out was I had been to school to be a patient care tech while I was pregnant with my son. I was a stay-at-home mom for two years while I was in school and of course, she knew about these degree changes too. She also knew about the many mlm companies I was involved in too. I've never been afraid of hard work and having multiple streams of income was always necessary while raising children.

Remember when I said this time was different. It was completely different all the way around. This time there was excitement when I said it. This time, I was sure of what I was saying and about to do. This time, there was no reason for me not to do what I was supposed to be working on six months earlier. I told my sister and my dad, and I was met with encouragement. No one seemed to be surprised but me. People will always see in you what you don't know is there. Playing catch up can be difficult sometimes, but it's also very rewarding.

"There is no greater gift you can give or receive than to honor your calling. It's why you were born. And how you become most truly alive" - Oprah Winfrey.

Notes

Chapter 4: What Now?

You've seen my journey. You have seen what I've gone through in order to get to this point. Let me reintroduce myself to you. My name is LaQuellis LaRae McGee, and I AM a certified life coach. Now that we have that out of the way let's talk about you, shall we? So I hope you've learned some valuable lessons from the twists and turns of my crazy life.

Nevertheless, let's go back and review the list that you made earlier. So, of the three things that you are good at and the thing you enjoy doing most, which one do you believe you were created to do? Is there one that sticks out more than others? Is there something on the list that people have told you should do for a living? It doesn't matter when you heard it. It doesn't matter if you ignore it up until now. Our goal now is to find it. If you're looking at the list wondering if these are really things you can do, then we need to keep digging. Take a moment and think. Do you have a background in customer service? Are you good at party planning? What field can you see yourself in from now on? What does complete and total happiness look like? When you close your eyes at night and your job is what you're thinking about, can you see what you're doing? You have to eliminate what you don't want to do in order to find out what you do want to do. I'm almost positive that you probably already know the answer to these questions. If you've had your revelations and ignored God as I have, then you probably already knew when you wrote the list.

We are called to do more than just walk this earth. We as Christians are supposed to show love, compassion, understanding, and forgiveness. We are to be the light in someone's life. Let your light so shine that men may see your good works and glorify your father, which is in heaven. You never know what a person may need. It could be a kind hug, listening ear, or even a friendly face. Be the light in someone's life. Show love no matter the circumstances. Walk side by side and hold someone up. You never know when you will need that same love you showed.

Now at this point, if you know what it is you should be doing, and it's on your paper, circle it. Put stars by it. This is it! You've been waiting for this moment. Take a moment and think about it. This is life changing. This is the reason you will get up and go every morning. This moment will give you brand new meaning. Take it in. Let's keep working. This is only the beginning. I can hear you now asking, what's next? What do I do? Well, the first thing you do is accept it. The calling on your life is sometimes too much for you to wrap your head around. However, this is your board game. This is your life, your calling. You have to be willing and ready to accept what God has created you to do. You can't still have questions. You can't still be walking in the dark. Now that you know what your calling is, it's time to grab the bull by the horns and be ready to work. But, where do you begin? Training! You have to have the proper tools in order to be successful. You aren't doing all this work to fail. Don't start out half stepping; jump in all the way around. And that's exactly what I did.

I went to training. While I was researching online and looking for the best place to get trained, I came across Fast Track

Coaching. I got confirmation online from a Facebook post. A young lady stated she was a life coach and this is where she got trained. I think the most attractive part to me was it required only one day to get it done. I didn't want it to mirror my time at school. This needed to be different because it is different. It means more than the degree I received in accounting. That was my choice. This one is God's choice. Don't think that you won't be met with opposition just because you've started a new path and journey. There will still be things to overcome. I tried going to class in April and May, but life happened. Nothing, in particular, it just had to be put to the side for a minute. Nevertheless, when the class came around in June, guess who was present? You're right, I was. And who would have ever guessed, that God would send an angel my way by the name of AJ. I went to Life training class, and she was my trainer. Her class was truly amazing. It was exactly what I needed to get going. She gave me all the tools that I needed on paper. She prepared me from a training standpoint, but I was already giving advice. I was already helping people make life-changing decisions. It was a matter of turning it into a business. There is a huge difference in talking to someone who trusts you and talking to someone who doesn't even know you exist. Both can be very challenging, but it's a part of the process.

This process has been a long time coming. There had to be changes in my personal life as well as my professional life, and there will be some in your life in many areas. That's the next step—Change. Some people had to be removed, and some added. Don't always look at change as a bad thing. Everyone isn't meant to go where God is taking you. Some people are there for a lesson. Once the lesson has been laid, they move on. It doesn't mean they didn't serve their purpose; it just means it's over with. Don't try to hang on, let go and be ok with the time that they were around. We make the mistake of going backwards, and that's not always in the cards. People who are supposed to stick around do. Some people you outgrow. Then there are those you should have let go long before now and those that shouldn't have been around, to begin with. I'm sure there was something there for you to learn from that connection. Take the lesson, but don't get stuck there. You can't move forward looking in the rearview mirror. The strides you've made don't mean anything if you're not using them to move forward. We seem to always fight this process of growth. So, let me be frank. GROWING PAINS HURT!

Why do you think they are called growing pains? See, for most people, you weren't the child that got the message when your parents spoke softly to you. Some of you had to be yelled at before you would get it. So, as an adult, when things become uncomfortable, you try to go back to where you were, and what you were doing when things were good. But, it's time for a change. It's ok to give yourself permission to be happy. Hmm, that one didn't strike you. Well, let me come into the room through another door. Do you think that you can be effective in what you're supposed to be doing if you haven't yet experienced that certain something in order to talk about it? If life has been a cakewalk, how would you be able to assist anyone with anything?

Life experience is also a good teacher. It's a painful teacher at times, but a good one. If you're not sure of things that need to change, let take inventory. Who are the most important people in your life? Who can you not live without? Why is this so important? What is your why? What is your long-term goal? What is your short-term goal? Once you've answered those questions, draw a line and under that line, write the names of the people who can help you achieve these things. Be honest. Again, not everyone is meant to be a part of this moment. I know you already know in the back of your mind that some people need to be removed, and it doesn't have to be an ugly thing. It can really be as simple as you are in a place in life where you need to concentrate on you. Being the best you, inventing the new you. Going to the next level and soaring among likeminded people. When changing your circle, you will be met with opposition. I've been met with the same, and it's ok. I don't expect anyone to be excited about my calling but me. I don't expect anyone to understand my purpose, but me. The crazy thing is those people who are going to be instrumental in your life and new walk will be excited. They will have nothing but positive things to say. They will understand that something is different. You won't have to tell them. They will be able to see it. Of course, in the midst of your excitement, you will tell them, but it will be good things to follow. Anything that is meant to hurt or harm you isn't for you.

Jeremiah 29:11 says, "For I know the plans I have for you," says the Lord. "They are plans for good and not for disaster, to give you a future and a hope."

The next thing you should be doing is surrounding yourself with people who are working in the field or area you're getting into. You're the newbie, but there is an expert in everything. You want to gain as much knowledge as you can. That's through conversations, books, seminars, etc. AJ has several Facebook live sessions. I'm unable to be on all of them, but I try to catch as many as I can. She is chop full of knowledge, and she shares so much valuable information on her lives, that it would be insanely crazy for me not to jump on. I have her book, and I'm waiting on the new one as well. I also have a book Dr. Duckett wrote. He is the creative mastermind behind Fast Coach Training. Who better to assist me in my journey than the man himself? With this being the age of technology, there is no reason you can't get knowledge daily. You want to be comfortable in what you're doing. You want to stand up straight and know what you're talking about and know what you're doing. People can smell fear, and they can tell if you're unsure. So show up for yourself the same way you have shown up for the previous bosses that you've had. You've helped them to reach their goals and build their dreams, now it's time to put the same energy and tenacity into your own.

    I know we live in a time where technology is the most popular thing going. The art of communication has changed so much. We send a text instead of making a phone call. We call instead of talking face to face, and oh, let's not forget the might world of social media. You have logged into your accounts just like I have and seen step by step what is going on day by day in a lot of people's lives. They post good morning, tell you about traffic, and then check in for lunch.

By the time three p.m. has rolled around, you've heard about the office conversation and what the boss did to make them mad. When we clock out, we have to hear about traffic again, but now the kids are involved and don't forget the picture of dinner. We are all guilty of it. And some stuff is newsworthy, but some stuff isn't. This particular topic isn't. You have to learn to move in silence. Not everything is meant to be told right away. Just like there are those praying for your success, there are also those praying for your downfall. Don't give them a front-row seat. Learn who to share things with. Who is on a need-to-know basis? What really has the keys to the kingdom?

If you have 1300 Facebook friends, I promise you not all 1300 are going to be excited about this. You also leave room for people to make comments and give their opinions. Does it really matter in this case? Now I know it shouldn't matter much at all, but there are those who are still looking for approval. They will never tell you, but they are. If you've hit a major accomplishment and you just have to post about it. Be vague. Change your emotions to feeling accomplished, and if that's not enough and you need the words, then say something along the lines of "it feels good to complete my task at hand". No one knows what you're talking about. That could simply be your things to do list for the day. It doesn't have to say I talked to my business coach today and decided to write a book and start new a business. Have you ever thought that what God shares with you is only for you to know at the time it's shared? When God speaks, does he need everyone to talk to you, or does he have a direct line? Move in silence.

I had one of my Facebook friends ask me what I had been doing. I hadn't been online in a while. I didn't tell him I was writing a book; it was not his business right now. I simply said, I had a lot going on and needed to take time to do some things. He said oh ok. Now does he have questions, I'm sure he does. However, he didn't ask, and I wasn't telling. He'll find out when this book is published. Not too many people knew I was writing this book. I pretty much only told my family and my best friend. Who else needed to know other than them? If we hadn't had this conversation before June 26, 2017, you were on the need-to-know basis, and this wasn't one of those times. I'm sure many will be surprised; I know I was when I got confirmation on it. But, it's ok. I'm not looking for approval, and I don't need it. I got the only approval I really needed when God spoke to me. Divine approval is much greater than man's approval. That connection is more important to me any day of the week.

Notes

Chapter 5: Setbacks

Remember when I said you would be met with opposition. I'm sure most people thought that to mean people, but that could be a lot of things. We could summarize those things as life, but I want to break that down a little more. Look at your paper. On the front of that paper, you have three things that you are good at. You also have your favorite thing to do. On the back you have things you want to accomplish and people who you think will be instrumental and assist you in doing that. Now, on another sheet of paper, we are going to discuss oppositions or Life. Name some of the things you feel will be oppositions. With the list of opposition, write one thing you can do to change it. It's hard to try to figure out what could go wrong. And truly that isn't where you want to spend most of your time and energy. But it needs to be on the table because it happens. So, there are three things we are going to deal with right now. They are you, age, and fear. I'm sure you're looking at that saying me? Yes, you. Are you surprised? It should be no shock that we are going to discuss this item first. I think we should clear the air on this one first before we move to the other two. We can talk ourselves out of anything. We are able to find every reason in the world to keep us from moving forward. We can truly be our own worst enemy.

"I can't change the direction of the wind, but I can adjust my sails to always reach my destination." - Jimmy Dean

Don't stand in your own way. You've done the hard part. Making the decision a change was needed and doing the work to find what you are supposed to do. Now it's time to walk in it. Don't go backwards. Don't look at what's been. Don't think about what could go wrong. Everything could go right. Don't be so afraid of succeeding that you sabotage yourself. It's so easy to look at something new and wonder if you're doing the right thing. You'll be met with opposition during the journey soon enough, therefore don't be your own opposition. When you look in the mirror, you need to encourage yourself, empower yourself, and build yourself up.

Highlight the phrases below and make them part of your daily talk to yourself.

"I can do this."

"I will be successful."

"I will soar high and make a difference in everyone's life that I come in contact with."

"I am unstoppable."

"I am unique."

"I will have what God has for me."

Speak life in yourself, your new business, and this new change. Words are powerful. Life and death are in the power of your tongue. What do you want to have? How do you plan to get it? Are you going to let anything or anyone stand in your way? These are things you must consider and always keep at the front of your mind.

The second thing on my list is age. Some people think, "I'm too old to make this change." I should have done this earlier in life. So what if you're 40 something, 50 something, or even 60 something. Life has happened. I know some people who were in their 70s when they got their high school diploma. Let that sink in. If someone who is 70 can go back and get their high school diploma, what is stopping you? Listen, you are never too old to make a change, especially one that will impact your life in a major way. Whoever said there was a time limit on anything that you can do other than the army? Life continues until God calls your ticket. If you let your age be a hindrance, what are you going to do in your older age? Don't wait around and let life pass you by. You are a vibrant, healthy person who is full of life. You are only as old as you act, not as you feel. Not letting your age become a stumbling block is another layer of an amazing story that has yet to be told. This new adventure you are on will not only open up new doors, but it gives you another chapter in this book of life. Making the decision was hard, and staying with it might be a little hard too. If it's worth having, it's worth fighting for.

> SUCCESS DOESN'T JUST COME AND FIND YOU, YOU HAVE TO GO OUT AND GET IT.
> —KUSHANDWIZDOM

The third opposition item is fear. We look at the opportunities to reinvent ourselves and start a new as a bad thing. But why is it a bad thing? If we are looking for new direction and a new beginning, doesn't that mean we have to start somewhere? You can't have it both ways. If you could go to sleep as an executive assistant and wake up a CEO, don't you think everyone would be changing careers? If it was as easy as saying this is what I want, then what's stopping the world from doing it? The fear of starting over is real, but it's also in your mind. When you do anything, there has to be a plan. There has to be something in place in order to know where you're going. Organization is the key to success. You can't make an excuse; that is the fear talking. Fear has two meanings: Forget everything and run, or Face everything and rise. What are you going to do? Don't let your mind and the things around you control you. You are in control of you and your destiny. Embrace it. This is life changing. This is exciting.

> **"THE FEARS WE DON'T FACE BECOME OUR LIMITS."**
>
> — Robin Sharma

Notes

Chapter 6: I'm Still Searching. It's Ok To Say No

I've talked about those of us who have found their calling, but some may not have found theirs. Let's chat for a minute. Let's review your list. If the three things that you're good at don't make you want to work in them every day, you have three other things that you are good at. Take a look at your favorite thing to do? Would you want to make a job out of this? These four things describe your personality and what you like. But there could be many reasons you haven't found your purpose. We get job after job. We continuously go to school obtaining degrees in a different area on a regular basis. We can't ever seem to find what we are looking for. Have you ever considered that you haven't found your purpose because you haven't asked God? I mean think about it. If anyone asks you a question, don't you give an answer? So let's be honest for a second. Our problem is, and yes I'm guilty of it too, we ask God, and he gives us an answer, but since we don't like it, we said we didn't hear it. No is an answer just like yes is an answer. God doesn't always have to let you take the long route. Yes, there are things that God arranges, and there are things the God allows to happen in your life. But on the flip side of that, there are things that God will prevent and things that God will not allow to take place in your life. If you really think about it, that's a good place to be grateful. Can you imagine what God has prevented in your life? And I'm not speaking of the small things. Imagine being on your way to work and you are stopped by every traffic light that you come to. Once you are on the interstate, you are still moving slow, but as you are driving, you notice emergency vehicles on the side of the highway. That could have been you. You could be waiting for an ambulance, police officer, or worse because you were the one involved in the accident. Everything has a rhyme and reason. So be patient, take your time. We get so wrapped up in timetables, what other people think we should be doing and by when, but we haven't taken the time to see where we really are. When are you getting married? When are you going to have a baby? Don't be a copycat. Don't look at what others have and think you want the same thing or you're supposed to have the same thing.

Everyone isn't supposed to be a millionaire. Somebody will be financially stable. Someone will be at peace that they have enough to do the things they are required every 30 days and still have room for some things that they want to do. Everyone isn't going to be as successful as the next person, even if you're doing the same thing. The purpose and calling on your life is just for you. No one can be you or do what you do. God only created one you! Even if you have children and grandchildren, there is still only one you. Yes, they have traits that we pass along, but that adds to who they are and who they become. That doesn't change them into you. Know that you are special. Walk with your head held high, your feet firmly planted, and ready to take on whatever comes your way. Take it on with power and authority. People will see in you what you see in yourself. No matter if that is good or bad; people see what we show them.

On your piece of paper, write down what you're showing people. Be honest and open. Do they see you being indecisive? Would someone use the word assertive to describe you? What do you see when you look in the mirror? What needs to change? While you're changing what you're doing, it's going to create a change in you. One you might not have seen coming, or one that you know should have taken place before now. The things that we engage in will have an effect on every aspect of your life, no matter if it's good or bad.

NEVER LET THE THINGS YOU WANT MAKE YOU FORGET THE THINGS YOU HAVE

I know if I ask you to name something you want you could do it without thinking about it. But, if I ask you to name a blessing can you do it without using the "regular" ones. Yes, God woke you up and protected you. But what else?? We get so hung up on our wish list that we forget the blessings we do have. Yes, he will give you the desires of your heart but how does that overshadow what he's already done? Hmmm, don't forget what you do have because what you want might not be what you need!! God keeps doing great things for you and me! Bless him for that, and the other will come!

If you haven't found your purpose, start positioning yourself to find out what it is. Your purpose won't be something that you're unable to do. If you've never been athletic, your calling isn't to be a pro athlete. That my friend is a dream and that is certainly different from your life's purpose. Dreams are a good thing, but your dreams may not always be your reality. It's always been a dream of mine to sing professionally. I've received offers to sing in different groups, but I know in my heart that my voice belongs to God. I'm not singing anything other than for Jesus.

Now in saying that, that doesn't mean that God will never honor my request, what that means is I know who I am, and I have to be and do differently than others. There is nothing wrong with being different. We are all uniquely created to be an individual.

Remember when we talked about the people around us, well we are here again. The people around us impact every aspect of our life. But while you're changing who you're with, you also have to change where you go. Both of these things can be grouped as repositioning. I have friends that have been in my life since grade school. We don't talk on a daily basis, we don't get together for lunch, but I know they are there. Just because we're friends doesn't mean that we have to be around each other all the time. That doesn't mean that I don't care or we won't ever talk. It simply means that life has taken us down different paths. I'm not so attached that I'm willing to sacrifice myself for them. We get in our feelings about losing certain relationships with certain people. Remember when I told you there are seasons, reasons, lifetime relationships, and people. Yeah, apply that here. Stop having so much loyalty to your past that is holding you bondage. Pronounce the benediction and release yourself. The only person that is holding you back is you. The only person that can stop you is you. You may be your own worse critic, but you're also the only one that can keep you from your destiny.

You could also have conversations with people or hire a life coach! (Yes, I'm available). When choosing a person to talk to, make a careful and informed decision. What do I mean? Well, you want to surround yourself with like-minded people. If you want to be successful, then you want to be around successful people. You don't want to be with the person that gives you the reason everything won't work. It's ok to play devil's advocate, but that is different from a Debbie Downer. Someone who doesn't have dreams, goals, and ambitions themselves so they can't get excited about a new something. They can't support you in what they don't have or see in themselves. Think about this. Every little girl has sat down and planned their life from who they will marry, to how many children they will have and their names. Where they will live, what they will do for a living, even including the car and the house. However, the 8-year-old you and the 38-year-old you don't look through the same glasses. The 38-year-old you has had life experiences, both good and bad. The 38-year-old you is looking for something that the 8-yearold you could never even imagine. So when you look at your paper now at 38, you're looking for things like stability, both financial and emotional. You want to build a future. You are thinking about career goals with short-term and long-term goals. You probably would like to go back and talk to the 8-year-old you to prevent some of the lessons you had to learn.

As time goes on, your picture changes as you grow older. You become more mature and think differently, so you adjust. You're not stuck in one place and flexibility is key. The next thing you should do is consider how serious you are about finding your purpose? Is this really what you're ready for? Don't bite off more than you can chew. You have to be in a place mentally, that you're ready to tackle this. What are some of the signs you should look for? You're tired of being impacted at work by lay off. Are you ready to start over? Are you having problems in your relationship because you aren't mentally present? You are always worried about money or other things that are going on because of the lack of satisfaction that you get from your current job. You're tired of working for someone else, or you hate your boss. Is your money funny and change a little strange? Are you looking for something that is recession proof? Are you unsure of your future? Are you determined to live a richer and fuller life? All of these questions will point you in a direction. If you can say that more than three of these questions apply to you, it's time for a change. It's time to hit the reset button. I challenge you to take inventory of the things that you do on a regular basis. Look at the things you enjoy. Your purpose is staring you in the face. You may also want to use my next book called *30 Days of Peace, Restoration, and Revelations* to assist you with finding your inner peace. It will give you a straight line to what you're looking for.

I know sometimes complaining about what's going on around me sounds better than actually doing something about it. I've always said I know it won't or didn't change anything, but I felt better about it once I finished. That's a lie. Complaining feeds into the fears that you already have. It tells you what you can't do and what won't work. But we give Satan credit for being busy. When will you learn? Satan isn't busy. Some of y'all do the work for him, and he sits back and watches you have a meltdown just like God does. Why would he need to be busy? You're doing a bang-up job for him. He's not worried about your meltdown. He's worried about those who are praying and asking God to lead and direct them. He's trying to figure out how to knock them down. How can I shake them to their core? When life deals you lemons, make lemonade. When you're stuck and don't know where to go or what to do? Pray and talk to God. Satan can only do what God allows him to do. This is still God at work. He knows what lessons we need to learn and who to put in our path, so we do. Don't give Satan an inch. Pray and praise your way through. You already know the outcome, so thank God today for your victory tomorrow!!!

Chapter 7: What Have We Learned?

You watch people daily and see that what they're doing and you know they are doing what they are supposed to do. You can see the excitement. There is never a dull moment in their lives, and they just ooze it all over. And you say to yourself I *want that! I want to feel like that! I want to feel like that about my work, about my job, and about my life.* And it's not that you're wanting their life, you want the part of their life that gives you satisfaction in what you're doing. When you find your purpose or your gift, it opens up so many opportunities, and you're filled with such joy and completeness. Can you sit back and imagine your life with clarity? Living a life with meaning? Having a life with peace? For some, they feel like it's unreachable, but everyone can have that. You can have that. You can find what it is that makes you wake up and go. It's not just your motivation; it's who you are. It's a part of you and your chemical make-up.

Look at your list again, and let's answer these four questions.

    1. Can you see yourself doing this every day?

2. Can you see yourself making money doing this?

3. How do you feel doing it?

4. Do you get satisfaction in doing it?

I know I get complete satisfaction helping others and giving advice. I'm the oldest of all my siblings, and that's what I've been doing for a very long time. My children's friends come and talk to me, which I take very seriously. I know I am helping to mold a young person into an adult that is getting ready to enter the world. I know I am good at what I do. I know I can help anyone who calls me for help. There has not been on time where my answer has been I can't help you. I don't know. Let me ask someone else. This is my calling, and I walk with my head held high in the air because I know who I am and what I am. That is the confidence you should have and exude. When you tell people what you do, they should be able to see it on you. If you tell someone I am a cook, and they didn't know you could cook, something might be a little off.

When you find that thing that is all about you, it's going to show.

For some, it's not going to be an easy process. Don't get discouraged, and don't be afraid to try things to find what you're good at. If you wanted to be a caterer, take a cooking class. Start cooking more at home. If you get burned out, and it doesn't do it for you, try something else. Is helping people what you've always enjoyed? Put together a community opportunity to help others. You will be able to see things first hand and understand the process of what needs to be done. You'll be able to pick a particular area, age group, and so forth. This will also let you know if you're up for the task.

One of the main things to remember is this is your life we are discussing. We are talking about what you're going to do every day for the rest of your life. It shouldn't be hard. It shouldn't be a task. It should be very easy and bring much joy and excitement.

"A person often meets his destiny on the road he took to avoid it."
– Jean de la Fontaine.

Meaning sometimes we do back into it, but sometimes it's on purpose. Failures are going to happen. They are a part of life, but they can also be part of your success. Don't let them define you. You're much more than that. Let it be a lesson, and learn from the lesson. It's a building block, a stepping-stone. It's one stop on the train to success. Milton Hershey filed bankruptcy before he made it big. No, I'm not encouraging you to file bankruptcy; I'm saying there are some hard backstories to the successful ones of some very famous people that we know. That should encourage you and let you know people don't always get it right the first time.

The only thing that beats a fail is a try. Be inspirational, be motivational, but most of all, be YOU!

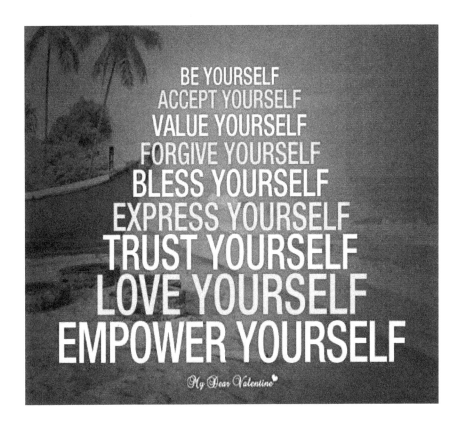

Conclusion

In the beginning, I told you we would dig deep inside to find what your purpose is. I hope you were able to move past some of the baggage life has left you with. I hope you have been able to have vision and clarity over areas in your life that may have been a struggle. The process of finding your God given purpose can take you down many roads. But only you know if they were a left turn. Only you know if it was a road that could have been avoided. Even if it could have been, you still learned a lesson while traveling. I challenge you to make positive strides forward. Hire a life coach that will help you move forward and higher.

If you haven't found your purpose, I challenge you to make some life decisions and set some goals. Make some realistic deadlines. If you want to really know what your purpose is, after you have figured out what you don't want to do, give yourself a time frame. Do you want to know within the next 90 days? And don't get discouraged when life happens, it's going to happen. And since we can't prevent it from happening, embrace the challenges and obstacles.

Everything will work together for your good.

Remember your goal is to Live Life On Purpose.

A Look Into The Future

Now it's time to do the work. Go to my website and sign up for our newsletter. It will come out once a month and have loads of information that will helpful on your journey. You can also schedule an appointment. We do virtual or remote as well as in person appointments. We believe in working through all barriers.

Every month in 2018, we will be advertising, promoting and selling The Power of Purpose in a city near you. Check our websites for scheduled events. Look for the audio version to be released by the end of January 2018. For booking engagements, you can email me at pixielee@bizzybossymommy.com

The next book is scheduled for a summer release. It's a 30 day devotional and the title is 30 days of Peace, Restoration and Revelation.

Follow us on Instagram and Twitter: @bizzybossymommy

Like our facebook page: www.facebook.com/bizzybossymommy

Website: www.bizzybossymommy.com

Phone# 770-548-2006

Email: pixielee@bizzybossymommy.com